DOES GOD HEAR ME WHEN I PRAY?

Written by: Lakisha M. Buckley

Illustrated by: Elena Yalcin

DOES GOD HEAR ME WHEN I PRAY?

Written by: Lakisha M. Buckley
Illustrated by: Elena Yalcin

DEDICATION

First and foremost I would like to thank my Heavenly Father who is my life. He makes all things possible.

This book is dedicated to my parents, Beverly Warren and the late Wilfred Jackson - without them there is no me.

To my husband Christopher Buckley - my biggest supporter. Thanks for believing in me and pushing me to be my best.

To the late Dr. David B. Gates - My Pastor who pushed me to work my gifts. Our last conversation sticks with me and pushes me to be all that God has called me to be.

To Apostle Phyllis Young and my Pastor Jacqeline R. Gates - thanks for your prayers and support throughout the years. This is the year of ELEVATION, PJG!

To my nieces and nephews: Jonea, Jania, Janice, Josiah and Jayden. Thanks for inspiring me to be the best version of myself. I love y'all.

To my Aunt Zelda, who inspired me to dream from a young girl.

To my entire family - thanks for your constant love and support.

Lakisha M. Buckley

My name is Elyse and sometime
I wonder, does God hear me when
I pray. I'm a curious young girl,
does he care what I have say?

Or when I whisper the words from my mouth, does he really care how they come out?

Or would he rather that I shout?
He's so far above the clouds,
in order for him
to hear me,
do I have to
speak or scream
out loud?

Can I think about what I want to say in my mind? If I chose to do that, would it still make him proud? Does it have to be a special way, and should it be every day?

Do I have to bend my knee, or can
I pray anywhere, like under a tree?
Where does it have to take place?

Or could it be in any space?

Does he really hear?
I mean, like with his EAR?

Should I pray for everyone, or should I be the only one? What if I pray too long? Tell me, God, would that be wrong?

What if I forget one day? Would that make him mad
and cause him to stay away? No, I dont think so!
God's nice and gentle in a fatherly type of way.

I love to pray only for my mother,
but I think I get it now;
I should pray for another.

I know I asked already, but does
he really hear me, and should
I only pray when I am sleepy?
Can I pray any time of the day?
And if the answer is yes,
can I pray in my own special way?

God, do you really hear me
when I pray? I often wonder:
Do you care what I have to say?

Then I remember what Mom
taught me about the bible.
She says it's the Holy Word,
and I would find the answers
to all I need to know.

It says that I should pray
each and every day.
Well, those are my words;
the bible says ALWAYS.

It also says that God will hear me when I call and that this is not just for me but for us all. He cares what we say and what we do, and guess what I found out? He LOVES me, too.

So now that I know he hears me when I pray, now I promise to pray to my God every single day.

ABOUT AUTHOR

Lakisha Buckley was raised in Freeport, NY. Being creative has always been at her core. As a young girl, she has always loved writing short stories and poems. Her desire has always been to write children's books and now she gets to live her dream.

She is a wife, loving aunt and faithful and loyal friend to many. There is never a dull moment with Lakisha - to know her is to love her. Her joyous spirit and infectious laugh bring joy to many.

Lakisha has a Associates' degree in Social Science and is currently a student at Old Westbury pursuing her Bachelors' degree.

www.ingramcontent.com/pod-product-compliance
Lightning Source LLC
LaVergne TN
LVHW072058070426
835508LV00002B/156